W9-BMP-891

Sandra Day
O'Connor

Sandra Day O'Connor

Lawyer and Supreme Court Justice

JEAN KINNEY WILLIAMS

Ferguson Publishing Company
Chicago, Illinois

Photographs ©: AP/Wideworld: 10–11, 24, 31, 52, 66–67, 70–71, 73, Neal Ulevich 95, 96–97, 98; Archive: 61; Corbis: 16, 19, 27, 78; Liaison: 44, 55, 58, Alan Day 62, 80–81, 82–83, 87.

An Editorial Directions Book

Library of Congress Cataloging-in-Publication Data
Williams, Jean Kinney
    Sandra Day O'Connor: lawyer and Supreme Court justice / by Jean Kinney Williams.
      p. cm.—(Ferguson's career biographies)
      Includes bibliographical references and index.
      ISBN 0-89434-355-6
      1. O'Connor, Sandra Day, 1930- —Biography—Juvenile literature. 2. Women judges—United States—Biography—Juvenile literature. 3. United States. Supreme Court—Biography—Juvenile literature. [1. O'Connor, Sandra Day, 1930- . 2. Judges. 3. United States. Supreme Court—Biography. 4. Women—Biography.] I. Title. II. Series.
KF8745.O25 W55 2000
347.73'2634—dc21
[B]   00-0337614

Printed in the United States of America
X-8

CONTENTS

Sandra Day
O'Connor

FROM COWGIRL TO SCHOOLGIRL

THE UNITED STATES Supreme Court building covers an entire city block in Washington, D.C. With sixteen massive white marble columns, its entrance looks like an ancient Greek temple. A flight of wide, marble steps leads up to the front door. On October 5, 1981, a crowd lined those steps to see a woman seated among the nine Supreme Court justices for the first time in the nation's history.

Sandra Day O'Connor became a national celebrity from the moment she was nominated to the Supreme Court. First she had

O'Connor and Chief Justice Warren Burger (both at center) were joined by her family on the day she was sworn in to the Supreme Court.

been a county judge, and then a state judge in Arizona for several years. President Ronald Reagan had promised to appoint a woman justice to the U.S. Supreme Court if given the chance. He considered several women to be nominated when Justice Potter Stewart decided to retire in 1981. After meeting with Sandra Day O'Connor for the first time, Reagan knew who his choice would be.

O'Connor was a Republican like Reagan, but she was also a woman who thought for herself. She had worked hard in the 1950s and 1960s to earn government positions usually denied to women, and she cherished her role as a wife and mother. Reagan, a California rancher himself, couldn't help but like the fact that O'Connor had spent much of her childhood as a cowgirl on a dusty ranch in the Arizona desert. He was intrigued by her background, which included rounding up cattle on horseback, shooting coyotes, and scholarship. She attended Stanford University when she was sixteen and graduated from law school near the top of her class at twenty-two. And when she was forty-two, she was the first American woman to become a state senate majority leader. As a judge in Arizona, O'Connor was considered tough but fair and open-minded, and she controlled her courtroom.

The U.S. Senate easily approved her nomination to the Supreme Court in September 1981. The beautiful courtroom of mahogany and marble where she was sworn in as a Supreme Court justice was a long way from the small adobe house in the Arizona desert where her life began.

Life on the Lazy B
The ranch had been in the Day family since Henry Day, Sandra's grandfather, claimed the land in the Arizona Territory in the 1880s. Henry Day had left Vermont and traveled west to start a new life. He

made some wise investments in lumber and real estate in Kansas and married a young Kansas woman, Alice Edith Hilton. Then Henry heard about the huge, low-priced tracts of Indian land the U.S. government was selling in the Arizona Territory after the Civil War. Day and a partner used his investment earnings to start a ranch. His partner bought several thousand head of cattle in Mexico and drove them across the U.S. border near the Gila River in what is now southeastern Arizona. The cattle were already branded with a *B* that appeared to be lying on its side, so the 300-square-mile (777-square-kilometer) ranch was called the Lazy B.

Henry's son—Harry Day—was born on the ranch in 1899. Only twelve years earlier, Apache Indians, led by the famous chief Geronimo, had raided area ranches, including the Days' ranch. They had lost several dozen horses. The ranch was isolated, so Henry Day built a one-room schoolhouse for his and other local children. Eventually, however, Henry and Alice moved to Pasadena, California, so that their children could go to a better school. They left the ranch in the hands of a manager.

As a young man, Harry Day had planned to attend Stanford University, near San Francisco in

Palo Alto, California. But when his father died suddenly, Harry learned that the Lazy B had money problems. Instead of going to college, Harry Day went back to Arizona to put the Lazy B back on its feet.

Harry came to know the Wilkey family of El Paso, Texas, through his cattle business. Romance soon bloomed between him and the Wilkeys' daughter, Ada Mae. She was a college-educated girl who loved high fashion, had traveled in Europe, and was an accomplished singer and musician. Nevertheless, after Harry and Ada Mae eloped in 1927, Ada Mae left her cultured, comfortable home behind to rough it on the Lazy B. Her new home, a four-room adobe house, had neither indoor plumbing nor electricity. Ada Mae had to cook, clean, and haul water for herself, her husband, and the ranch hands. Their first child, Sandra Day, was born in 1930.

Little Sandra spent the first several years of her life with no playmates her own age. However, she was at home in a world of horses, cowboys, shotguns, wildcats, and coyotes. Her backyard stretched to the horizon. When Sandra wasn't tagging along with her father on his chores, Ada Mae read to her. She read newspapers, books, and magazines such as the *National Geographic* to Sandra, until she was five years old. By then, Sandra could read them herself.

School in El Paso

By 1935, with no schools near the ranch, Harry and Ada Mae decided to send Sandra to El Paso to live with her grandparents, Mamie and Willis Wilkey. There she would attend school, only returning to the Lazy B in the summer. "We missed her terribly, and she missed us, but there was no other way for her to get a good education," her mother said. Sandra's grandfather Willis died when Sandra was in third grade, leaving her grandmother alone to take care of Sandra and her cousins. In later years, Sandra said her grandmother "was a wonderful person— very supportive of me. She would always tell me that I could do anything I wanted to do. She was convinced of that, and it was very encouraging."

Sandra became close friends with her cousin Flournoy Davis, who also lived with Mamie Wilkey. They attended the private, all-girls Radford School, which had small classes and encouraged independent thinking. Sometimes, just before their lunch break, girls were given topics to discuss in front of their class immediately upon returning. This taught

Young Sandra (right) with her mother (left), brother Alan (on lap), and sister Ann (in center). As a child, she divided her time between Arizona and Texas.

them to gather their thoughts and express them with very little preparation. One of Sandra's favorite teachers stressed the importance of public speaking. At Radford, young Sandra practiced a variety of skills she would use later in her life. Her teachers considered her very bright, and she was advanced a grade, graduating from Radford at age twelve.

Summer School

When Sandra was eight years old, her sister Ann was born. By the next year she had a brother, Alan. After her grandfather died, her grandmother spent summers at the Lazy B with Sandra's family, and Flournoy often came too. Summer was a wonderful time for the girls. Sometimes they rode horses to swimming holes and fished with hooks made from safety pins. Other times they explored Cottonwood Canyon along the Gila River and studied the pictures carved into the rock by Indian tribes long ago.

Sandra and Flournoy spent many summer days playing cards, and reading books. Sometimes they turned the Days' front porch into a stage and put on a play for the ranch hands. Even something as simple as getting a shipment of ice for the icebox was a welcome event. (People kept food cold in iceboxes before electric refrigerators were invented.) The huge chunk of ice that was delivered to the ranch was too big to fit into the icebox so it was shaved and chipped until it fit, and the shavings were used to make ice-cold lemonade or ice cream. Sandra's summer schooling consisted of learning to shoot coyotes, prairie dogs, jackrabbits, and Gila monsters. By the time she was eight, Sandra could drive a tractor and rope cattle. Though they lived miles from the nearest neighbor, Ada Mae taught her oldest daughter social graces. Sandra knew how to cook for—and entertain—a large gathering. Meanwhile her father would engage Sandra in political discussions. As the Day children grew older, family vacations might mean a trip to Alaska, Mexico, or Cuba. The summer Sandra was fourteen, Harry and Ada Mae "packed us into the car and we drove to every state capital west of the Mississippi. We climbed to the dome of every capitol building until finally we had to come home," recalled Sandra's brother, Alan.

Summer's end was always a sad time for Sandra. Much as she loved her grandmother, she always longed for her family and life at the Lazy B. One year, when it was time for her and Flournoy to return to El Paso, the girls were swimming in the

Sandra at age ten. She spent many happy summers on the Lazy B Ranch in Arizona.

ranch's water-storage tank when her father came to get them for the trip. They refused to come out, and Harry Day had to retrieve them with a lasso! Another year, her parents allowed her to attend the nearest school, which was 22 miles (35 kilometers) away in Lordsburg, New Mexico. But the daily traveling was so long and exhausting that Sandra returned to El Paso the next year.

By age twelve, Sandra was a student at Austin High School in El Paso. Even as a young girl, "Sandra always knew how to handle herself," said one of her high-school friends. Sandra took honors classes and showed her skill for impromptu speaking, "but she also did all the normal things teenagers did—had crushes and talked about boys," as her friend said years later. "She was just never loud or awkward. She really could do everything well." Sandra graduated from high school at age sixteen and was the only student in her class who planned to attend college. Her one choice was Stanford University in California, the same school her father had wanted to attend. Though she was only sixteen years old and was competing against thousands of soldiers just back from World War II, Sandra was accepted. Some people in those days felt women should stay at home and allow soldiers returning from the war to have the best jobs or attend the best universities. In spite of this attitude, Sandra insisted upon attending Stanford. It would not be the only time she would ignore such obstacles.

THE LAW, MARRIAGE, AND MOTHERHOOD

THOUGH SHE WAS younger than her classmates and female students were in the minority, Sandra did well at Stanford. It was considered an Ivy League college for westerners, which meant its classes were challenging and its students were the top high-school graduates in the United States.

Female college students of the time often studied "women's" subjects such as education or English, but Sandra decided to major in economics. Her first-year roommate recalled that "Sandra was never afraid to

At Stanford. Sandra Day proved to be a determined college student and majored in economics.

speak up in class," even though women were out-numbered at Stanford. She took a class on business law, which had a particularly interesting teacher, and was drawn to the idea of attending law school. Sandra took part in a program that allowed students to finish their senior year of college while starting their first year of law school. Sandra was one of 7 women out of 150 students in her law class. She received her bachelor's degree from Stanford magna cum laude, meaning "with high honor." Among her law-school classmates was William Rehnquist, another graduate whose future destiny was a seat on the U.S. Supreme Court.

Law school teaches students to think on their feet and to be ready for unexpected questions. In ancient Greece, a great teacher named Socrates taught his students by asking them questions and making them aware of the various points of view on a subject. Sandra's law professors used the same approach, called the Socratic method, in teaching law. They questioned students about cases they were studying. The key to success in those situations is to be as familiar as possible with a case and with the law and legal theory behind it. It was also an important part of Sandra Day O'Connor's success throughout her life. She used these methods in law school, politics, and with her family. "I think that anything you do in life requires preparation," she said many years after graduating.

At the Top of the Class

Sandra was named a member of the distinguished Order of the Coif, a national honorary legal society. She was also chosen to be an editor of the *Stanford Law Review*, another honor awarded to top law students. Because they are responsible for all of the material that eventually ended up in the law review, editors spend many long hours in the law library doing research and making sure that all of the information in the articles is accurate. Another law review editor who often joined Sandra Day in the university library was John J. O'Connor III, a student who was a year behind her in law school.

Sandra didn't spend all her time studying while she was at Stanford University Law School, though. She enjoyed going to drive-in restaurants and weekend dances with her friends. She also would sometimes her law school friends to the Lazy B for a visit. Sandra liked to take college friends home for roundups. These roundups consisted of counting and sorting all the thousands of head of cattle that roamed the many thousands of acres of the vast Lazy B ranch. Sandra and her university friends enjoyed saddling their own horses and working like cowboys.

Sandra Day (first row, second from left) with the other editors of the Stanford Law Review. *Being a member of this group was a high honor.*

Sandra's closest friends during law school were her housemates at Cubberly House, also the home of the widow of Stanford's dean of education. Mrs. Cubberly rented rooms to female graduate students, who took turns cooking meals.

In the spring of 1952, shortly before she graduated from law school, Sandra began dating John O'Connor, her coeditor on the law review. She found him to be not only an able law student but a good dancer with a wonderful sense of humor. Their romance became serious, and they set a date for a wedding at the Lazy B. Her parents liked him when she took John home to the ranch for the first time, but her father joked later that he'd "seen better cowboys."

Women's Work?

In the meantime, Sandra graduated from law school. Though she ranked third in her class and had been a law-review editor, she was unable to find work as a lawyer in a law firm. Very few lawyers in the early 1950s were women, and many of them had jobs in firms owned by male family members. Now Sandra's hard work and achievements seemed to count for nothing. She could seldom even get an interview. At last, she was offered a job as a legal secretary, but she turned that offer down. Had she taken it, she might have met the future attorney general of the United States, William French Smith, who was a young attorney in California at the time. One day he would help recruit Sandra Day O'Connor for the Supreme Court in Washington.

She finally accepted a job as a law clerk in San Mateo County, working for the district attorney. She was finding that government was an easier area to break into as a professional woman than private companies. She did legal research and wrote opinions on cases, staying close to John O'Connor, who was in his last year of law school. That December, Sandra and John were married at the Lazy B in front of the fireplace in her parents' living room, which was packed with family and friends. After the wedding ceremony, guests gathered in the barn for the reception. Pine branches brought down from the mountains decorated the rafters for the Christmas wedding, and bales of hay provided the seating. Sandra's college friends danced with cowboys to the music of a local band, and Lazy B barbecued beef was served for supper.

Sandra continued working as a law clerk while John finished up at Stanford. He was drafted into the army shortly after he graduated in 1953, and became a member of the Judge Advocate General's Corp, a legal branch of the army. The O'Connors were sent to West Germany. Sandra also applied for a legal job in the army—and she was hired. From 1954 to 1957, she worked as a civilian lawyer for the Quartermaster's Corps in Germany, which bought supplies and food for the troops. Her job was to read all the contracts. Sandra and John toured Europe while they were stationed in West Germany. They also spent three months skiing in the Austrian Alps when John's tour of duty was finished. When they had spent all their traveling money and had a baby on the way, they decided it was time to return home.

Settling In

Home, the couple decided, would be Phoenix, Arizona, which was the state capital and in the same part of Arizona as the Lazy B. To Sandra, her home state was a "land of opportunity and happiness," as she later described it. Air-conditioning had become more available in the 1950s, making hot climates more comfortable, and Phoenix was growing.

Sandra and John spent the summer of 1957 studying for the state bar exam, a test they had to

Phoenix in the 1950s. The O'Connors decided to settle there and start a family.

pass in order to practice law in Arizona. Whenever possible, they studied around the pool at their apartment. They became friends with Tom Tobin, another law-school graduate who was also studying for the bar exam. All three of them passed. John began working for a law firm and, three days after she was sworn in to the bar, Sandra gave birth to the O'Connors' first child, Scott Hampton. The fact that the O'Connors had passed the bar exam together was considered quite unusual, and a local newspaper featured a photograph of Sandra, John, and baby Scott.

The O'Connors settled easily into their Phoenix community—John becoming active in local Republican politics and Sandra working with Tom Tobin in his small law firm. Sandra worked half-days, staying in the office in the mornings until Tobin arrived in the afternoon. The cases they handled varied from drunken-driving charges to landlord-tenant disputes. They did "whatever business we could get to come our way," as Sandra O'Connor said later. Sometimes they were paid by the state to represent prisoners who couldn't afford a lawyer. Those assignments didn't pay much, but they gave Sandra and Tobin valuable courtroom experience.

After the O'Connors' second son, Brian, was born in January 1960, Sandra gave up practicing law for the time being to concentrate on motherhood. By May 1962, the O'Connors welcomed a third son, Jay. Sandra was an active mother. The O'Connor boys took swimming lessons, learned to ski with their parents, and, like their mother, learned to ride horses and rope cattle at the Lazy B. As much as O'Connor loved her profession, she considered her family the most important part of her life. Later, when she first became a judge and performed marriage ceremonies, she would tell the couples that "marriage is the foundation of the family, mankind's basic unit of society, the hope of the world, and the strength of our country."

The O'Connors built a new home in what became a fashionable and wealthy neighborhood just north of Phoenix, giving their house a traditional southwestern touch by soaking some of the adobe bricks in skim milk before they were baked. Arizona was growing tremendously. The many affluent newcomers meant an increase in business for law firms such as the one John O'Connor worked for, and government jobs also became more available, which would eventually benefit Sandra.

As her children grew, Sandra kept busy with volunteer projects. She organized a lawyer-referral plan for the local bar association, which helped people find a lawyer when they needed one. She volunteered in a school whose students were black and Hispanic, and she worked for the YMCA and the Phoenix Historical Society. Volunteer work was important to her, she later said, because it helped her get to know her community better. Volunteering was also her way of trying "to make it [the community] a good place to live." Like her husband, Sandra became involved with Republican politics. She served on the Governor's Commission on Marriage and the Family and worked on campaigns for Republican candidates. Among her friends, she counted not just community leaders and politicians, but also people like a ranch hand at the Lazy B who came to Phoenix for medical treatment, alone and sick.

The Proving Ground

When Jay turned three years old, Sandra, at age thirty-five, decided to turn her attention back to working. Her two older sons were in school, and she wanted to work part-time so that she could take them to school in the morning and pick them up in the afternoon. Once again, she didn't have an easy time getting a job. But after many calls to the Arizona state attorney general's office, she was finally hired part-time.

As an assistant attorney general, she represented agencies such as the Arizona State Hospital for the Mentally Ill and the Arizona Children's Hospital. She represented them in court, lobbied for them in the state legislature to pass laws that might help them, and advised them on state laws. She enjoyed her experiences in court, and asked for more assignments involving court appearances. Gradually, her part-time hours became full-time. She became known for her knowledge and accuracy in legal matters, and newspaper reporters occasionally quoted her when reporting on state-government issues.

Sandra Day O'Connor's involvement with the Republican Party would prove to be good timing on her part. Arizona had been in the control of Democratic lawmakers for several decades. But in 1966 a Republican governor was elected, and both the Arizona state senate and the house of representatives were controlled by Republicans.

When the state senator from the O'Connors' district accepted a job working for President Richard

Nixon in Washington, D.C., it left an opening in the state senate. The Republican Party had to choose someone to fill that position until the next election.

They chose one of their hardest-working and most professional members—Sandra Day O'Connor. O'Connor's fast-moving career took a new turn.

HER FIRST "FIRST"

S A CHILD ON her parents' ranch and as a young student in El Paso, Sandra Day O'Connor learned to work hard. She was prepared for just about anything, from an impromptu speech at Radford School to a court case in Phoenix. Early in her legal career, when women lawyers were a rarity, she learned to be persistent— she never gave up.

However, by the mid-1960s, more women were entering professions that had been dominated by men. The civil rights movement and the idea of an Equal Rights

Amendment for women were becoming important social issues in America. As a result, Sandra Day O'Connor's sex was less of a barrier when she returned to her professional life. But O'Connor's career wasn't everything. As one of her friends said, she "understands very well the conflict between a woman's desire to be part of the professional world and yet to be a perfect mother and wife, as well."

Stepping into the Senate

When she was first appointed to the Arizona state senate, O'Connor described herself as "a fiscal conservative and a moderate Republican." She believed that government should be careful in spending taxpayers' money and that all Americans should be treated equally and fairly under the law.

Like many Republicans, O'Connor opposed gun control and the forced busing of students to integrate schools. She also helped reinstate the death penalty. On the more liberal side, she supported bilingual education in Arizona, because the number of Spanish-speaking citizens was growing quickly. She helped pass a strict antipollution law and supported accident insurance for migrant workers. She also believed that reporters who didn't want to disclose their sources should be protected by law. She favored laws requiring government agencies to hold more public meetings that citizens could attend, and she worked to increase and improve services for the mentally retarded. She also helped pass laws that provided regular reviews for people committed to mental institutions.

Though O'Connor was generally conservative, she didn't just automatically vote with other Republican senators. She studied each issue carefully before deciding how to vote. For example, she was criticized by other Republicans and the Phoenix newspaper the *Arizona Republic* for helping write a family-planning law that would have made birth control available to anyone who wanted it. She believed the law would help cut down on the number of abortions in the United States. And she was opposed to using state funds for private schools, even though her sons attended a private school.

Leading the Majority

After her first year in the state senate, O'Connor had to run for election. In 1972, she was easily re-elected, winning the second-highest number of votes among the state senators; the district she rep-

An exterior view of Arizona's state capitol

resented had become the biggest in the state. When O'Connor returned for her third term, the Republican senators chose her to be the senate majority leader. Her new position made national news: she was the first woman to be chosen as majority leader in any state legislature in the United States. Her new responsibilities were to gather support for proposed laws, or bills, important to the Republicans and to keep Republican senators voting together on bills. She also organized the committees that studied the issues lawmakers voted on. O'Connor would learn as much about each issue as possible to convince other senators so that when a bill came up for a vote, it would pass.

One colleague described her as a "super floor leader," while another called her "extraordinarily tough." One of her Democratic opponents, Alfredo Gutierrez, had to admit her leadership was effective. "It was impossible to win a debate with her. . . . She would overwhelm you with knowledge," he said. *Time* magazine wrote about her history-making position as a senate majority leader, noting her devotion to detail, such as the time she wanted to change a bill by adding a comma. Some of O'Connor's colleagues felt she tried to exercise too much control.

"She was as hard-nosed as they come in a floor fight, tougher in committee meetings, and absolutely ruthless in caucus—behind closed doors," said one of her opponents.

Equality for All?

In 1972, O'Connor introduced the Equal Rights Amendment (ERA) for approval by the Arizona senate. The amendment to the U.S. Constitution had been approved by Congress and would have prohibited national laws from treating men and women differently. In order for the amendment to become law, at least thirty-eight state legislatures had to ratify it by June 1982. O'Connor said she supported the ERA because "women have lacked a certain amount of job opportunity and have failed to receive equal pay for equal work." But she couldn't get the Arizona legislature to pass it. Two years later, she tried to put the issue before Arizona voters, but that effort also failed. After 1974, O'Connor focused instead on individual laws she felt discriminated against women. (The ERA died because only thirty-five states had ratified it by the 1982 deadline.)

O'Connor also led the repeal of a state law barring women from working more than eight hours a day to "protect" them—though even the state government ignored that law—which passed in the senate by just one vote. She also worked to make property and divorce laws more fair to women, since men in Arizona still had the power to control and manage property owned by a husband and wife. O'Connor also fought sexual discrimination against girls by pushing through a state law allowing girls as well as boys to receive financial loans from the state for agricultural projects.

Because of her prominent position in a male-dominated field she was often invited to speak to women's or student groups. She would stress the responsibility of individual citizens to know about their government and to participate in it by voting. Amid her attempts to have the ERA added to the Constitution, O'Connor remained a champion of the importance of strong marriages and families. She served on the board of her children's school and enjoyed spending time at home with her family when the senate wasn't in session.

After five years as a highly visible state politician, Sandra Day O'Connor announced that she would not seek reelection to the Arizona senate in 1974. She'd realized, she said, that she wanted to

In 1974, O'Connor was elected to the position of trial judge on the Maricopa County Superior Court.

"get back into the mainstream of the law." As one of her senate colleagues said, "She had to choose between politics and the law. She was more comfortable with the law." Other colleagues wondered if O'Connor's perfectionism made it difficult for her to be a lawmaker, where compromise is more important.

O'Connor Goes to Court

Ready for a different challenge, O'Connor decided to run for a position as a trial judge on the Maricopa County Superior Court. Sticking to her theme of the importance of family and community, she campaigned "as a citizen, a wife, and a mother." The growing city of Phoenix had one of the highest crime rates in the United States, so law and order was another issue O'Connor ran on. Her goal as a judge, she told voters, would be to "help replace fear in our streets with strength in our courtrooms."

She won the election, defeating a man who had been appointed temporarily to the judgeship three months earlier. As a lawyer, Sandra Day O'Connor had enjoyed her experiences in court. Now she was headed back to court, but this time it would be her courtroom.

FROM THE STATEHOUSE TO THE BENCH

THE SCENE WAS an Arizona courtroom. A mother of two small children had been found guilty of writing several thousand dollars' worth of bad checks. The woman pleaded for probation, which would have kept her from going to prison, and the judge's response was, "You have intelligence, beauty, and two small children. You come from a fine and respected family. Yet, what is depressing is that someone with all of your advantages should have known better." When the judge announced a prison sentence of five to ten years, the young woman cried out, "What about my babies?" The judge hurried from the courtroom and fled to her chambers, or office, where she broke down in tears. That case, said Sandra Day O'Connor, was her most difficult as a trial judge. The young woman sentenced to prison that day was actually released after eighteen months, but the case was a good example of the judicial style of Judge Sandra Day O'Connor, who didn't believe in coddling criminals or leaving wrongdoing unpunished.

She didn't coddle prosecutors, defense lawyers, or anybody else in her courtroom either, where she handled cases dealing with murder, rape, burglary, fraud, drug peddling or possession, and divorce. As a trial judge, O'Connor had the last word in the courtroom. She presided over the opposing lawyers and gave instructions to the jury. If there was no jury, she decided on a defendant's guilt or innocence and imposed a prison sentence if necessary.

Still Prepared

As a lawyer and legislator, O'Connor learned the value of preparation, both in arguing the law and in making it. She spent much time reading outside the courtroom to catch up on trends in the law or to prepare for upcoming cases. When she became a trial judge, lawyers appearing before her learned the importance of preparation, too. O'Connor was a stickler for facts and decorum—or proper procedure—in her courtroom.

"You have to say something awfully funny to get her to smile on the bench," said one lawyer. Poorly prepared lawyers who appeared before Judge O'Connor got little sympathy. If they asked for more time on their case, they would have to explain why, often to their embarrassment. She was even known to advise a criminal defendant to fire a lawyer who wasn't doing a good job. Lawyer Alice Bendheim said it was no use trying "to snow her" with arguments not supported by facts. On the other hand, said one public defender, John Foreman, "if a lawyer was well-prepared and all business, she was pretty easy to get along with." Foreman found O'Connor to be "fair, persuadable, and open-minded."

Sworn to uphold the law, O'Connor expected prosecutors and police to honor it too. Though she made her share of mistakes and saw some of her rulings overturned by the state supreme court, she wasn't afraid to hand out tough decisions to defendants and prosecutors alike. In one case, she had imposed a death sentence on a convicted criminal but reversed that decision and ordered a new trial when it was discovered that the prosecuting attorneys had withheld important evidence at the trial. And in her zeal for law and order, she wouldn't allow important evidence to be brought out in a trial if the police didn't obtain it legally.

As she heard more cases, O'Connor became more open-minded as a judge, and would consider a defendant's circumstances or what she might perceive as their potential, even if they'd made a mistake. She sympathized with a battered wife convicted of shooting her husband and gave her the shortest sentence possible. O'Connor then wrote to the governor to ask that the sentence be reduced even further. In another case, a young man was convicted of dealing heroin and selling stolen property. She believed she saw something promising in him and gave him a light sentence and probation. Eventually, he earned a college degree and had a successful business career.

Governor O'Connor?

In 1978, after O'Connor had spent three years as a trial judge, Republican leaders in Arizona approached her about running for governor. Her friend and supporter Arizona senator Barry Goldwater also encouraged her to run. But after carefully considering the idea, O'Connor decided against it. It would be an expensive campaign, she reasoned, and difficult to run for the highest office in the state while she performed her duties as a judge. The Democratic candidate, Bruce Babbitt, was elected governor.

In 1979, Governor Babbitt asked O'Connor to fill an opening on the state appeals court. Some suggested that Babbitt offered Sandra the job so that she wouldn't run against him in the next governor's election. But Babbitt said, "I had to find the finest talent available. Her intellectual ability and her judgment are astounding."

In most states, there are three levels of courts: the trial, the appellate (or appeals), and the supreme court. The federal courts are similar, with the United States Supreme Court being the highest. In Arizona, Sandra O'Connor was one of nine state appeals court judges who heard cases that had already been to trial. The cases were being appealed to a higher court because one of the parties involved disagreed with the court's decisions.

Governor Bruce Babbitt appointed O'Connor to the Arizona state appeals court in 1979.

The nine judges worked in groups of three. O'Connor and two other judges spent one day each week listening to lawyers argue why a previous decision should or shouldn't be overturned. The rest of the week was spent researching the law involved in those cases and writing their opinions—their decisions on the case. Sometimes decisions were unanimous among the three judges; sometimes it was a two-to-one split. In either case, one judge was chosen to write the opinion.

O'Connor herself wrote twenty-seven opinions. Usually the cases were not as exciting as those she heard as a trial court judge. Her appeals court opinions dealt mainly with divorce settlements, landlord-tenant disputes, appeals from criminal trials, bankruptcies, or business lawsuits. One of her opinions, for example, favored tenants in a dispute with their landlord who, by state law, could require the tenants to pay two years' rent up front in order to avoid eviction from the apartment. That law, O'Connor wrote, discriminated against poor tenants.

O'Connor was as businesslike in the courtroom as she had been as a trial judge. Arizona lawyers who rated judges around the state considered O'Connor accurate and attentive to legal matters, but said she was lacking in "courteousness to the litigants and lawyers." One lawyer who considered O'Connor to be aloof and arrogant was surprised to get a phone call from her. O'Connor was asking for help in intervening on behalf of "two people in jail who shouldn't be there." Sandra had heard about their situation through her volunteer work at the Salvation Army and had the family of one of the prisoners in her office. O'Connor still kept a busy volunteer schedule. She also helped the local historical society and the Heard Museum, served as a trustee of Stanford University, and organized a state association of women lawyers.

Another Opportunity

In 1980, O'Connor also became involved in a legal exchange between England and the United States. Judges from each country observed the legal and court procedures of the other. At that time, O'Connor became acquainted with U.S. Supreme Court chief justice Warren Burger, another American judge participating in the exchange.

Ronald Reagan was then running for president. One of Reagan's campaign promises was to put a woman on the Supreme Court if elected. One of

In London. Warren Burger first met O'Connor when they both participated in an exchange program with British courts.

O'Connor's friends remarked to her, "Sandra, maybe you'll be it." "Well, thank you for thinking of me, but that would just never happen," said Sandra. O'Connor was happy with her position on the Arizona state appeals court. She pictured herself and John spending the rest of their days "in our adobe house in the desert," as she said. A new job and a move across the country seemed very unlikely—until early summer, 1981.

Another Arizona appeals court judge, Donald Froeb, remarked to a reporter that O'Connor "always assumes the leadership role." In 1981, the leader of the United States sought her out and, at the age of fifty-one, with all her children graduated from high school, O'Connor considered another challenge.

THE PRESIDENT COMES CALLING

N MARCH 1981, Justice Potter Stewart told Vice President George Bush that, after twenty-three years on the Supreme Court, he planned to retire. Sandra O'Connor was busy in her chambers one day in early July when she received a telephone call from President Ronald Reagan. Reagan said he planned to nominate her to fill the vacancy on the Supreme Court.

Soon, secret service agents and the White House press secretary arrived in Phoenix, followed by television and newspaper reporters and photographers. Sandra tried calling her parents, but the phone was out of order. Harry and Ada Mae first heard of their daughter's nomination when President Reagan announced it himself on television. Once the word was out, Sandra was showered with congratulations and publicity. When Mayor Margaret Hance of Phoenix tried to call O'Connor to congratulate her, it was impossible

Meeting with the president. O'Connor was nominated to the Supreme Court by President Ronald Reagan.

to get through on the phone. She had to send a telegram instead!

A Woman on the Court

Women's organizations had been lobbying for a woman on the Supreme Court since Lyndon B. Johnson's presidency in the 1960s. Though Johnson had been given the names of three potential female judges for the Court, he appointed his friend Abe Fortas in 1965. President Richard M. Nixon ap-

President Lyndon Johnson with his Supreme Court nominee Abe Fortas

pointed justices Lewis Powell and William Rehnquist, Sandra's law-school classmate, and Gerald Ford put John Paul Stevens on the bench. Jimmy Carter would have liked to appoint a woman to the Supreme Court, but there were no vacancies during his presidency.

During the 1980 presidental campaign Reagan wasn't as popular with women voters as his opponent, Jimmy Carter. Reagan's advisors suggested that he make a major promise to women. When Reagan announced that he intended to appoint a woman to the Supreme Court, his support from women voters improved.

It wasn't clear that Reagan would make good on his promise once he was in office though. The only high-level woman in his administration was the U.S. ambassador to the United Nations, Jeanne Kirkpatrick. And out of the forty-one federal judges Reagan appointed, only one was a woman. But when Reagan learned of Potter Stewart's retirement, he had his staff draw up a list of women from whom he could select a potential replacement. By the end of June, the choice was narrowed to four candidates: a state supreme court justice from Michigan, two federal judges, and Sandra Day O'Connor.

Jeanne Kirkpatrick, U.S. ambassador to the United Nations. When Reagan took office, she was the only woman with a high-level position in his administration.

In the saddle. O'Connor and Reagan shared a love of horses and life on a western ranch.

While narrowing down their choice, Justice Department lawyers flew to Phoenix to interview O'Connor. In her favor was her acquaintance with Supreme Court justices William Rehnquist and Warren Burger. She also had worked hard for the Republican Party, and her views on issues such as law and order, the death penalty, strong families, and the role of the federal government in everyday life were much like Reagan's. Though not all of her colleagues over the years liked her style or agreed with her, O'Connor seemed to have no political enemies.

As she was being considered for the nomination to the Supreme Court, O'Connor went through interview after interview with Reagan's staff. She answered every imaginable personal question. "We were testing her psychological and intellectual stamina," one staff member said later. O'Connor impressed them on both counts. Her last interview was with the president.

A Meeting with the President

Sandra reminded Reagan that they'd met when both were politicians in Arizona and California, trying to get state spending-limit proposals on the ballot. "Yours passed, but mine didn't," Reagan commented, and they discussed their mutual love of ranch life. Their meeting lasted forty-five minutes. Afterwards, Reagan was convinced that O'Connor was the person he wanted to nominate for the Supreme Court.

There was some negative reaction to her nomination from groups who wanted a Supreme Court justice who was against abortion, but overall public reaction to her appointment was positive. Though O'Connor was a Republican and conservative on many issues, the liberal National Organization for Women called her nomination "a major victory for women's rights." By the end of July, a public opinion poll showed only 6 percent were opposed to her nomination.

O'Connor had only a few weeks before she would have to go through yet another series of questions, this time by the Judiciary Committee of the United States Senate. If the committee approved her nomination, the whole Senate would then vote on her appointment. In the meantime, she had opinions she needed to finish writing for the Arizona appeals court and she had to study for her confirmation hearings. She knew that the senators on the Judiciary Committee would quiz her about the Constitution and the effect it has on a variety of legal issues, so she hired a staff to prepare background material for her to study. She also read recent Supreme Court decisions and word-for-word accounts of other confirmation hearings. While the Federal Bureau of Investigation (FBI), the American Bar Association (a lawyers' organization), and staff members of the Judiciary Committee did their own investigations of O'Connor, she spent her last week preparing before the hearings began in Washington. At home, phone calls had been so numerous that she had to leave town to finish her preparations.

Before the Senate

When the hearings finally began in September, O'Connor listened to the opening statements of the eighteen committee members, and then she made her own statement. She was honored, she told them, to be the first woman nominated to the Supreme Court. "I happily share the honor with millions of American women of yesterday and today whose abilities and whose conduct have given me this opportunity for service." She discussed her belief in the importance of state government, and in what she considered to be the different roles played by the three branches of the federal government. She

Meeting with Senator Barry Goldwater. Senator Goldwater of Arizona supported O'Connor's nomination to the Supreme Court.

expressed her view that the correct role of the judiciary was to interpret and apply law, not create it. She told the committee that she could not predict the way she would vote on matters that would come up before the Court, nor would she say which previous decisions she approved or disapproved of. She introduced her husband and their three sons as well as her sister and brother-in-law. Then it was time for the committee to begin their questioning.

The senators asked O'Connor about her views on the death penalty, the ERA, affirmative action, and the different roles of judges and lawmakers. Having been well prepared on these issues, O'Connor answered calmly and confidently. Many of the senators' questions concerned abortion, which has long been a controversial issue, especially since the Supreme Court decision in the 1973 case *Roe v. Wade* case. In that case, a Court majority decided that the Constitution provides for each person's privacy, including a woman's right to end a pregnancy, and that it is unconstitutional to ban abortion. Abortion opponents wanted each state to make its own abortion laws, and they were not pleased that O'Connor had defended abortion rights while she was in the Arizona state legislature. As O'Connor went through her confirmation hearings, abortion opponents demonstrated against her nomination outside the Senate Office Building.

O'Connor told the senators that she had "an abhorrence of abortion as a remedy" for unplanned pregnancies, but had voted to repeal Arizona's anti-abortion law in 1970 because she thought it was too vague. "At that time I believed some change was appropriate," she said in the hearings, but that her views toward abortion had "changed over the years" and in the future she might rule differently on that law. Nevertheless, she would not indicate how she would vote on that issue if it came up before the Supreme Court. This frustrated some of the senators. The abortion question came up again during the O'Connor's Senate Judiciary Committee confirmation hearings, but each time O'Connor's response was a polite refusal to answer.

She was also asked about her view of the court's role in society. She told the senators, having been a lawmaker herself, "I know well the difference between a legislator and a judge, and the role of the judge is to interpret the law, not make it." In an article O'Connor wrote for the *William and Mary Law Review*, she had expressed her belief that the federal

*Against O'Connor.
Many pro-life groups
demonstrated against
O'Connor's nomination.*

Sandra Day O'Connor answers questions before the Senate Judiciary Committee

court system should be taking fewer cases. That came up during her hearings with a question from Ohio's Senator Howard Metzenbaum, who thought U.S. citizens should have more access to federal courts. O'Connor defended her views, stating she strongly believed in the abilities of the state court systems to administer proper justice in most instances.

During the hearings, representatives of some women's organizations expressed their pleasure at O'Connor's nomination to the Supreme Court. When Senator Joseph Biden of Delaware told O'Connor that "You have an obligation to be an advocate for women," spectators at the hearing burst into applause. But O'Connor did not respond. As she told the senators, she wanted to be known for her work, not for her gender.

As the three days of questioning wore on, O'Connor's chances of winning approval from the Judiciary Committee seemed quite good. The American Bar Association recommended her as "qualified." *Time* magazine described her as "probably the most thoroughly prepared nominee in history." She had the support of Republicans and Democrats, and there was nothing major in her background or past performance to disqualify her.

O'Connor stood with Vice President Bush and others to celebrate her unanimous confirmation to the Supreme Court.

"The women of America would storm the Senate Judiciary Committee and trash it" if her nomination was rejected, predicted newspaper columnist Mary McGrory.

When it came time for the committee to vote, the result was seventeen to zero in favor of O'Connor; one senator, who was strongly anti-abortion, did not vote. A week later, the whole Senate had the chance to confirm the nomination. Senators took turns singing her praises for four hours, and the final vote was 99 to 0 (one senator was absent). O'Connor would be the first woman to sit on the Supreme Court of the United States.

Afterward, a crowd gathered to cheer O'Connor as she stood with Vice President Bush and Attorney General Smith on the steps of the Capitol, which looks toward the Supreme Court building. "My hope is that ten years from now, after I've been across the street at work for a while, they'll all be glad they gave me that wonderful vote," she told the crowd. Later, at a dinner hosted by South Carolina senator Strom Thurmond and his wife, O'Connor joked that "Thomas Jefferson and James Madison would be turning over in their graves right now, but let's hope that Abigail Adams would be pleased."

"THE MOST INFLUENTIAL WOMAN IN AMERICA"

"I, SANDRA DAY O'CONNOR, do solemnly swear that I will support and defend the Constitution of the United States." said the newest Supreme Court justice when she took the oath of her appointment on September 25, 1981. Each new justice takes two oaths: the first in the courtroom before hundreds of spectators, and the second one in the justices' private conference room with only the eight other justices. For O'Connor's swearing-in, some rules were bent.

Normally, the doors are closed when all the seats are filled, but to accommodate

Sandra Day O'Connor is sworn in as the first woman justice on the U.S. Supreme Court.

dozens of writers and courtroom sketch artists, additional people were allowed to stand. And President Reagan asked to be present at both historic events.

Upon her confirmation to the Supreme Court, O'Connor received thousands of letters, all of which she answered. A ten-year-old Massachusetts girl wrote that "I guess you find your job a proud one— I would." Another girl wrote instead to Chief Justice Warren Burger, not pleased with what she'd noticed on television—that Burger's robe went to his ankles, while O'Connor's was only to her knees. "I don't think that's fair," the girl wrote. "So if you get a long robe, so should she." Writing back to the girl, Burger explained that Justice O'Connor was still wearing her Arizona judge's robe, and would get a new one eventually. "They wear out after a while, especially in the sleeves," Burger wrote.

O'Connor's office, with its 15-foot (4.5-meters)-high ceilings and dark wood paneling, was warmed with family photos and leather chairs, as well as Navajo rugs and other Native American art objects that O'Connor brought with her to Washington. On her first day in court in October, John O'Connor was part of the crowd. He watched his wife take her place among the eight other justices, all seated

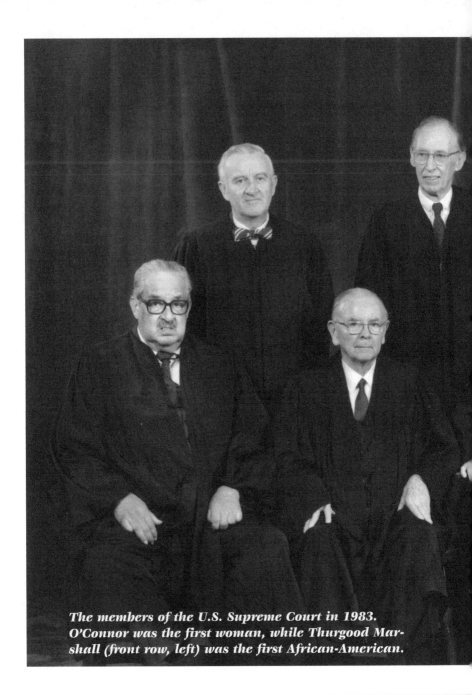

The members of the U.S. Supreme Court in 1983. O'Connor was the first woman, while Thurgood Marshall (front row, left) was the first African-American.

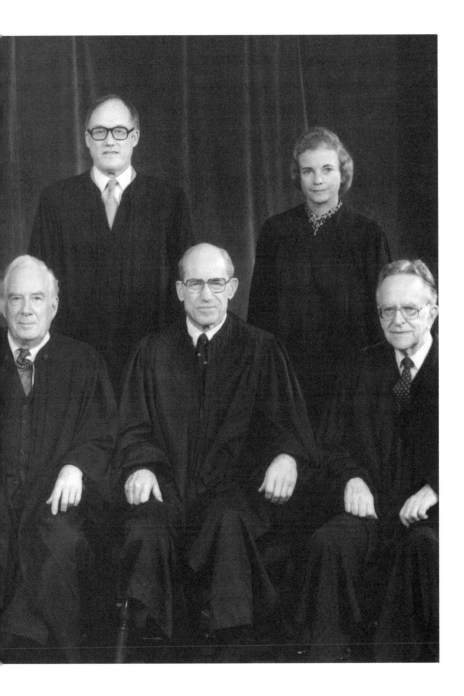

behind a long table facing the lawyers whose cases the Court had decided to review. The chief justice sits in the middle, and the associate justice who has been on the Court longest sits to the right of the chief justice. To the left sits the justice with the second-longest number of years at court. As the newest justice, O'Connor sat at the far left of the table.

How the Court Works

Each year, the Supreme Court receives about 5,000 requests to review cases, but the justices are able to hear only about 150. They choose these cases by vote; four votes is enough to bring a case to court. The judges gather in their conference room to discuss and vote on which cases to hear.

The Supreme Court justices have many cases to consider each year. They listen to arguments and then write opinions about their votes.

Once a case is selected for review, the lawyers involved are notified and a date is set for the oral arguments. Having already read the written arguments for a case, the justices listen to the lawyers' oral arguments in the courtroom, which is open to the public.

Between October and May, the judges spend two weeks every month listening to arguments for four cases each day. Lawyers for each side have thirty minutes to present their case. After hearing the arguments, the justices meet for a case conference, where the case is discussed and a vote taken on the decision.

When a majority decision is reached by at least five justices, one is chosen to write the opinion—an explanation of the decision. A justice who disagrees with the majority decision might choose to write a dissenting opinion, telling why that justice thinks the majority opinion is incorrect.

"Writing opinions is a justice's single most important task," said former Supreme Court clerk Peter Huber in his book about Sandra Day O'Connor. A Supreme Court opinion must be clearly understood, because it often sets a new legal standard that other judges and legislators will have to follow.

Some Court observers try to guess how the justices will vote by noting the questions and comments made during oral arguments. However, the outcome of a case remains a closely guarded secret until it is announced. In an average term, O'Connor may write from fifteen to twenty majority opinions, and perhaps as many concurrences—separate majority opinions—or dissenting opinions.

O'Connor's first opinion was easy, because all nine justices agreed that an organization could not sue the U.S. Department of Energy. The organization could not sue, wrote O'Connor, because the secretary of energy had acted within the law in question.

Another of O'Connor's opinions concerned the case *Rose v. Lundy,* in which O'Connor wrote for the 8–1 majority that the state courts could have been better used in deciding the case, establishing the "total exhaustion" rule, which says that a case shouldn't be heard by the Supreme Court until all lower courts have been tried.

O'Connor was considered very conservative in her first year at court. *Time* magazine called O'Connor "Rehnquist's Arizona twin," because the two of them voted the same way on twenty-seven out of thirty-one cases. But, as was often the case with O'Connor before she arrived at the Supreme Court, she was always unpredictable. For example, she sided with liberal justices and wrote the 5–4 majority opinion for a case, ruling it unlawful for a state university in Mississippi to exclude men from its nursing program.

In 1984, O'Connor wrote an influential concurring opinion in the case of *Lynch v. Donnelly*. The suit questioned whether a government-sponsored Christmas display was an unconstitutional endorsement of religion. The majority opinion favored keeping up the Christmas display, which included a Santa Claus figure as well as a nativity scene. The display was not "a message that the government intends to endorse . . . Christian beliefs," but rather "celebrates a public holiday," the Supreme Court said.

A year later, though, O'Connor joined a Court majority in declaring that a state government could not require schools to have a moment of silent prayer. O'Connor wrote that it encouraged prayer, which she believed went over the line separating church and state.

A Champion of Independence

O'Connor has consistently voted against random searches of high-school students for illegal substances, such as cigarettes or drugs. For example, a New Jersey high-school student sued her principal after he searched her purse for cigarettes. O'Connor joined the majority opinion stating that school

The U.S. Supreme Court in 1993. Another woman, Ruth Bader Ginsburg, was nominated to the bench in that year.

authorities should have "reasonable grounds" for such a search, or evidence that a search might turn up something. In 1995, she reached a similar conclusion when she voted against the drug testing that one school district required of all student athletes. She was not in the majority this time, and she wrote a strong dissenting opinion which said that "an overwhelming majority of [students in America] . . . have given school officials no reason whatsoever to suspect they use drugs at school."

Another former Supreme Court clerk, Edward Lazarus, speculates that O'Connor's western upbringing, in which she learned independence, contributes to her decision-making as a judge. For example, she tends to vote against broad affirmative action as in the case *City of Richmond v. J. A. Croson Co.* O'Connor wrote the opinion for that 1989 case and said that when a government sets aside a percentage of contracts for minority businesses, it goes against equal protection of all citizens as guaranteed by the Constitution. On the other hand, she was in favor of affirmative action in a 1987 case in which female plaintiffs showed that the Santa Clara (California) County Transportation Agency had no history of hiring women in certain positions.

In her years on the Supreme Court, the death penalty has been one issue O'Connor consistently votes for. She believes the death penalty may be imposed on both juvenile and mentally handicapped convicted murderers. Regarding abortion, O'Connor is in the middle. Abortion cases come up continually before the Supreme Court, as groups for and against abortion struggle to influence the issue. Since the Supreme Court called abortion a constitutional right in 1973, it also decides how far government can go in restricting it.

While O'Connor has stopped short of voting to overturn *Roe v. Wade*, she criticized it from the bench and voted in favor of laws banning abortions in publicly funded hospitals. She has also ruled in favor of laws forbidding use of government money to counsel women toward undergoing an abortion. She ruled that a minor (someone under the age of eighteen) should not have to get permission from both parents to undergo an abortion, because so many children's parents are divorced that locating both parents wouldn't always be possible. On the other hand, she favors at least one parent being notified, as she voted in another case. She also upheld a law requiring women to wait at least twenty-four hours after confirming their pregnancy before having an abortion, and a requirement for doctors to give information about abortion to women before they have one.

The Supreme Court in 2000

O'Connor has proved to be an influential member of the Court, as she is often considered the swing vote in many of the Court's 5–4 decisions. O'Connor and her colleague Anthony Kennedy often find themselves somewhere in the middle of the conservative and liberal judges, though in the last decade the Court has swung back to conservatism in issuing narrow 5–4 decisions. The seven other Supreme Court justices are:

- John Paul Stevens, who will turn eighty in the year 2000, his twenty-fifth year on the Supreme Court. Appointed by Republican President Gerald R. Ford, his decisions have become increasingly liberal over the years. He dissents from conservative decisions regarding affirmative action and separation of church and state.
- William Rehnquist, who was appointed chief justice by Reagan when Warren Burger retired in 1986. Rehnquist, born in 1925, was considered

the most conservative member of a liberal court when he joined it in 1972.

- Antonin Scalia, appointed in 1986 at age fifty, is often distinguished by his sharp-tongued opinions. For example, when a majority of justices, including O'Connor, voted to admit women to the all-male Virginia Military Institute, Scalia said such liberal opinions are "not the interpretation of the Constitution, but the creation of one."

- David Souter was appointed by Republican President George Bush in 1990. Like Stevens, his decisions have become increasingly liberal over the years. He has voted in favor of affirmative action and a powerful federal government.

- Clarence Thomas was born in 1948 and is the second black judge to sit on the court. He was appointed by President George Bush in 1991 after the retirement of Thurgood Marshall, the first African-American on the Supreme Court. He is a consistently conservative voter, very much against abortion.

- Ruth Bader Ginsburg was appointed by President Bill Clinton in 1993. Like O'Connor, Ginsburg graduated at the top of her law-school class, but was unable to find a job in New York City law firms in the 1950s. Instead Ginsburg became a clerk for a federal judge. She was also known as an activist for women's rights. As a Supreme Court judge, she generally votes along liberal lines.

- Steven Breyer, who became the newest member of the Court in 1994 at age fifty-seven, was appointed by President Bill Clinton. His views are generally liberal on issues such as affirmative action, the power of the federal government, and separation of church and state.

Issues before the Court

One of the most important issues the court is considering during its 2000–2001 term is Miranda rights, named after the defendant in the original case. Since a 1966 Supreme Court decision, anybody arrested in the United States is supposed to be told his or her rights by the arresting officer. The Fifth Amendment to the Constitution says that criminal defendants don't have to incriminate themselves, or testify against themselves, so the Miranda rights remind anyone under arrest that they don't have to make a confession if they choose not to. If a prisoner makes a confession without being told of his or her Miranda rights, that confession can be thrown out in court. Congress passed a bill two years later, in 1968, stating that if Miranda rights are not read to a prisoner at the time of arrest, it doesn't mean all of the evidence collected up to that point must be thrown out. The court will decide the constitutionality of the law this year.

Another case the Court has agreed to hear could affect children who attend religious schools. The justices will decide if taxpayers' money can be used to buy computers and other educational materials for those schools. Justice Stevens called it "A hard line to draw," but he isn't expected to vote in favor of tax dollars going to religious schools, nor is Souter.

Once again, O'Connor's and Kennedy's votes could determine the outcome, either way. Some consider this case to be a test case that could indicate how the justices would vote on the idea of families using tax vouchers to pay for the schools of their choice, including religious schools.

Justice O'Connor will turn seventy in the year 2000, but she shows no signs of slowing down. She was diagnosed with breast cancer in 1988 (as was Justice Ginsburg in 1999) and underwent surgery, but missed no oral arguments that term. She scheduled her cancer treatments for Fridays, so that she could rest on the weekends and still put in a full workweek.

Behind the Scenes

Each justice has four clerks who act as assistants. They are law-school graduates and have already worked as clerks for a federal judge. Their Supreme Court job lasts one year, and it is a high honor to be hired. The clerks help their particular justice by gathering information for cases that have been accepted or for which an opinion is being written. They also summarize the thousands of case requests that come before the Court each year, helping the justices decide which cases to hear.

The justices and their clerks work sixty to seventy hours a week and can become quite close. O'Connor remembers her clerks with a cake on their birthdays, and occasionally brings in a Mexican lunch on a Saturday afternoon, or schedules "field trips," such as an afternoon exploring one of the many museuems at the Smithsonian Institute or even a white-water rafting expedition.

On one rafting trip she organized, the rafting

Time away. John and Sandra Day O'Connor enjoyed a vacation to China in 1987.

Talking with a Comanche chief. O'Connor appreciates the time she gets to spend with different kinds of people.

The Sovereignty Symposium

CHARLES
CHIBITTY

FACUL

Justice O'Connor considers her job to be both an honor and a great responsibility.

guide told the group the most important rule: If someone falls from the raft, everybody else must stay aboard. But when it was O'Connor who fell off the raft, all her Supreme Court clerks jumped in the river to save her and got quite a scolding from the guide. But, as one of her clerks said later, "If you are clerking for Sandra O'Connor, you aren't going to be the one to let her drown. Her other clerks, and a few million other people besides, would never forgive you!"

At the time of her appointment, one women's magazine called O'Connor "the most influential woman in America." The Supreme Court, after all, can collectively overrule the president or Congress. But, as O'Connor said in 1981, "I think the important thing about my appointment is not that I will decide cases as a woman, but that I am a woman who will get to decide cases."

Since half of all law-school students today are women, as she said a few years ago, there should be even more women on the Supreme Court. In the meantime, Sandra Day O'Connor relishes "working with my talented colleagues on the most challenging legal issues in the country."

TIMELINE

1930 Sandra Day, first child of Harry and Ada Mae Wilkey Day, is born in El Paso, Texas.

1935 Though raised on her parents' ranch, the Lazy B in southeastern Arizona, lives with her grandparents when she was sent to school in El Paso, Texas, at age five.

1937 Lazy B gets electricity and indoor plumbing.

1938 The Days' second daughter, Ann, is born, followed in 1939 by Sandra's brother, Alan.

1942 Graduates from Radford School in El Paso,Texas, and starts high school in the fall.

1946 Graduates from high school and begins freshman year at Stanford University in California.

1950 Receives bachelor's degree from Stanford, and completes first year of law school; while in law school is selected to be an editor for the *Stanford Law Review* and is made member of Order of the Coif, a national honor society for law students.

1952	Graduates from Stanford Law School third in her class; is hired as a deputy county attorney; marries John J. O'Connor III in a December wedding at the Lazy B.
1953	Works as a civilian attorney for the army.
1957	Returns to Arizona and passes the state bar exam shortly before the birth of first son, Scott Hampton, in October.
1958	Practices law part-time with a partner.
1960	Son Brian is born.
1962	Son Jay is born; quits her law practice to focus on her three sons and her volunteer work.
1965	Returns to work as an assistant state attorney general.
1969	Is appointed to the Arizona state senate; runs for the position in 1970 and is elected.
1972	Wins reelection to the state senate, and is chosen to be the majority leader, the first woman given that position in any state legislature in the United States.
1974	Is elected to a state judgeship on the Maricopa County Superior Court, a position she holds for five years.
1978	Is urged by Republican colleagues to run for governor but decides against it.
1979	Is appointed to Arizona Court of Appeals by Governor Bruce Babbitt.

1981	Is nominated to the U.S. Supreme Court by President Ronald Reagan when Justice Potter Stewart retires; wins Senate confirmation by a vote of 99-0.
1988	Undergoes surgery for breast cancer
1999	Votes with the majority ruling that schools can be held responsible when students are sexually harassed by peers

HOW TO BECOME A LAWYER AND A JUDGE

The Job

Lawyers serve our legal system in two ways—as advocates and as advisors. As advocates, they speak for their clients. They represent the rights of their clients in trials, or in front of administrative and government groups. As advisors, they tell clients how the law affects the clients' business or personal decisions. Lawyers represent individuals, businesses, and corporations. More than 681,000 lawyers work in the United States today in all areas of law.

Judges are elected or appointed officials. They are in charge of federal, state, county, and municipal courts. They apply the law to citizens and businesses and oversee court proceedings according to the law. Judges also rule on issues that were not previously decided. More than 71,000 judges work in the judiciary section of the U. S. government.

All lawyers are qualified to give legal advice and represent clients in court. No matter what their specialty, their job is to tell clients their rights under the law and then help them exercise these rights before a judge, jury, government agency, or arbitration panel. In businesses, lawyers manage tax matters, arrange for stock to be issued, handle claims, represent the firm in real estate dealings, and give advice on all legal matters. For individuals, lawyers may serve as trustees, guardians, or executors; they may draw up wills or contracts; and they may advise on income taxes or buying or selling a house. Some work only in the courts; others carry on most of their business outside of court—by drawing up mortgages, deeds, contracts, and other legal documents, or by doing the background work necessary for court cases. For example, they might research cases in a law library or interview witnesses. Some lawyers work to establish and enforce laws for the federal and state governments by writing the laws, representing the government in court, or serving as judges.

Lawyers can also become professors in law schools. Administrators, research workers, and writers are also important to the profession. Many administrative positions in business or government are nonlegal in nature, but the background and experience of a lawyer is often helpful in such positions.

Some individuals with legal training may choose not to practice law but may have jobs in which their background and knowledge of law are important. These include tax collectors, credit investigators, FBI agents, insurance adjusters, process servers, and probation officers.

Some specialized fields for lawyers include the following: Civil lawyers work in a field also known as private law. These lawyers focus on damage suits and breach-of-contract suits; prepare and draw up deeds, leases, wills, mortgages, and contracts; and act as trustees, guardians, or executors of an estate when necessary.

Criminal lawyers are also known as defense lawyers. They specialize in offenses committed against society or the state, such as theft, murder, or arson. They interview clients and witnesses to get the facts in a case, compare their findings with known cases, and defend a client against the charges made. At the trial, they conduct the defense, examine witnesses, and summarize the case with a closing argument to a jury.

District attorneys are also known as prosecuting attorneys. They represent the city, county, state, or federal government in court proceedings. They gather and analyze evidence and review legal material relevant to criminal charges. Then they present their case to the grand jury. The grand jury decides whether the evidence is sufficient to prove an offense. If it is not, the lawsuit is dismissed and there is no trial. If the grand jury decides to charge the accused, however, the case goes to court. There the district attorney appears before the judge and jury to present evidence against the defendant.

Probate lawyers specialize in planning and settling estates. They draw up wills, trusts, and similar documents for clients who want to leave their belongings to their heirs when they die. Upon a client's death, probate lawyers vouch for the validity of the will and represent the executors and administrators of the estate.

Bankruptcy attorneys assist their clients in financial matters. They work for both individuals and corporations, in obtaining protection from creditors under existing bankruptcy laws and with financial reorganization and debt repayment.

Corporation lawyers give advice to businesses about their legal rights, obligations, or privileges. These lawyers study constitutions, laws, previous decisions, and all legal matters that affect corporations. They advise corporations about prosecuting or defending a lawsuit. They represent corporations in various business deals and seek to keep clients from expensive lawsuits.

Maritime lawyers specialize in laws regulating commerce and navigation on the high seas and any navigable waters, including inland lakes and rivers. Although there is a general maritime law, it operates in each country according to that country's courts, laws, and customs. Maritime law covers contracts, insurance, property damage, and personal injuries.

Intellectual property lawyers help their clients with patents, trademarks, and copyright protection. They include patent lawyers who secure patents for inventors from the United States Patent Office and prosecute or defend lawsuits of patent infringements. They may prepare detailed specifications for the patent, organize a corporation, or they may advise an existing corporation to commercialize on a patent.

Tax attorneys handle all sorts of tax problems. These may include problems of inheritance, income tax, estate tax, franchises, and real estate tax.

Insurance attorneys advise insurance companies

about legal matters. They approve the wording of insurance policies, review the legality of claims against the company, and draw up legal documents.

An international lawyer specializes in the rules observed by nations in their relations with one another. Some of these laws have been agreed to in treaties, while others have evolved from long-standing customs and traditions.

Securities and exchange lawyers monitor individuals and corporations involved in trading. They oversee their clients' activities to make sure they comply with the law. In takeovers and mergers, securities and exchange lawyers represent the corporations' interests and fulfill all legal obligations.

Real estate lawyers handle the buying and selling of property, search public records and deeds to establish ownership, hold funds in escrow accounts, and act as trustees of property. They draw up legal documents and serve in other capacities to aid purchasers and sellers in various real estate transactions.

Title attorneys deal with titles, leases, and contracts pertaining to the ownership of land, and gas, oil, and mineral rights. They prepare documents that cover the purchase or sale of such property and rights, examine documents to determine ownership, advise organizations about legal requirements, and participate in trials or lawsuits in connection with titles.

It is important to note that once you have a license to practice law, you are legally qualified to practice any one or more of these and many other specialties. Some general practitioners handle both criminal and civil matters of all sorts. To become licensed, you must be admitted to the bar of the state you work in.

Bar examiners test the qualifications of all law school graduate applicants. They prepare and administer written exams to the applicants covering legal subjects, examine candidates orally, and recommend the admission of those who meet the standards.

Lawyers become judges by either being elected or appointed. Judges preside over federal, state, county, or municipal courts. They rule on court procedure during trials and hearings and establish new rules when necessary. They read or listen to claims made by parties involved in civil suits and make decisions based on the facts, the law, and previous court decisions. They examine evidence in criminal cases to see if it supports the charges.

Judges listen to each case, rule on the admission of evidence and the testimony, and settle arguments between attorneys. They instruct juries on their duties and advise them of the laws that apply to the case. They sentence defendants found guilty of criminal acts and decide who is responsible in nonjury civil cases. Besides their work in the courtroom, judges also research legal matters, study previous rulings, write opinions, and keep up with laws that may affect their rulings.

A magistrate, or justice, is a judge who is not bound by constitutional and state regulations. Magistrates hear civil cases in which damages do not exceed a certain amount, as well as minor misdemeanor cases that do not involve prison sentences or fines over a certain sum.

Requirements

High School   A high-school diploma is a requirement. Courses in government, history, social studies, and economics are good preparation for college-level law courses.

Postsecondary   To enter a law school approved by the American Bar Association, you must complete at least three—and usually four—years of college. Most law schools do not specify any particular courses for prelaw education. Usually a liberal arts track is best, with courses in English, history, economics, social sciences, logic, and public speaking. A college student planning to specialize in a particular area of law, however, might also take courses related to that area, such as economics, agriculture, or political science. Those interested should write to several law schools to find out their requirements and whether they accept credits from the college the student is planning to attend.

At present, 177 law schools in the United States are approved by the American Bar Association; others, many of them night schools, are approved only by state authorities. Most of the approved law schools, however, have night sessions to accommodate part-time students. Part-time courses of study usually takes four years. Law-school training consists of required courses such as legal writing and research, contracts, criminal law, constitutional law, torts, and property. The second and third years may be devoted to specialized courses of interest, such as evidence, business transactions, corporations, or admiralty. Studying cases and decisions is of basic importance to the law student, who will be required to read and study thousands of cases. A degree of juris doctor (J.D.) or bachelor of laws (LL.B.) is usually granted upon graduation. Law students who are considering specialization, research, or teaching may go on for advanced study.

Most law schools require applicants to take the Law School Admission Test (LSAT), where prospective law students are tested on their critical thinking, writing, and reasoning abilities.

Licensing and Certification   Every state requires that lawyers be admitted to the bar of that state before they can practice. They require that applicants graduate from an approved law school and pass a written examination in the state in which they intend to work. In a few states, graduates of law schools within the state are excused from these written examinations. After lawyers have been admitted to the bar in one state, they can practice in another state without taking a written examination if the two states have reciprocity agreements. However, they must meet certain state standards of good character and legal experience and pay any applicable fees.

Other Requirements   Federal courts and agencies have their own rules regulating admission to practice. Other requirements vary among the states. For example, a few states allow a person who has spent several years reading law in a law office but has no college training or who has a combination of reading and law school experience to take the state bar examination. Few people now enter law practice in this manner.

A few states accept the study of law by correspondence. Some states require that newly graduated lawyers serve a period of clerkship in an established law firm before they are eligible to take the bar examination. Almost all judges appointed or elected to any court must be lawyers and members of the bar. Most have years of experience.

Exploring

If you think a career as a lawyer or judge might be right up your alley, you can find out more about it before making that final decision. First, sit in on a trial or two at your local or state courthouse. Try to focus mainly on the judge and the lawyer and take note of what they do. Write down questions you have and terms or actions you don't understand. Then talk to your guidance counselor and ask for help in setting up a telephone call or interview with a judge or lawyer so that you can ask your questions and get the scoop on what those careers are really all about. Also talk to your guidance counselor or political-science teacher about joining a shadowing program. Shadowing programs allow you to follow a person in a certain career around for a day or two to get an idea of what goes on in a typical day. You may even be invited to help out with a few minor duties.

You can also search the World Wide Web for general information about lawyers and judges and current court cases. Read court transcripts and summary opinions written by judges on issues of importance today. After you've done some research and talked to a lawyer or judge and still think you are destined for law school, try to get a part-time job in a law office. Ask your guidance counselor for help.

Employers

About 70 percent of the more than 681,000 practicing lawyers in the United States in 1998 were in private practice, either in law firms or working alone, according to the U.S. Department of Labor. The rest had government jobs, mostly at the local level. The majority of lawyers working for the federal government held positions in the Departments of Justice, Treasury, and Defense. Lawyers also hold positions as house counsel for public utilities, transportation companies, banks, insurance companies, real-estate agencies, manufacturing firms, welfare and religious organizations, and other businesses and non-profit organizations.

Starting Out

The first steps in entering the law profession are graduation from an approved law school and passing a state bar examination. Usually, beginning lawyers do not go into solo practice right away. It is often difficult to become established, and additional experience is always helpful to the beginning lawyer. Also, most lawyers do not specialize in a particular branch of law without first gaining experience. Beginning lawyers usually work as assistants to experienced lawyers. At first they mainly do research and routine work. After a few years of successful experience, they may be ready to go out on their own. Other choices open to the beginning lawyer include joining an established law firm or entering into partnership with another lawyer. Positions are also available with banks, business corporations, insurance companies, private utilities, and with a number of government agencies at different levels. Many new lawyers are recruited by law firms or other employers directly from law school. Recruiters come to the school and interview students. Other new graduates can get job leads from local and state bar associations.

Advancement

Lawyers who have outstanding ability may expect to go a long way in their profession. New lawyers generally start as law clerks, but as they prove themselves and develop their abilities, they find many opportunities for advancement. They may be promoted to junior partner in a law firm or establish their own practice.

Lawyers may enter politics and become judges, mayors, congressmen, or other government leaders. Top positions are available in business, too, for the qualified lawyer. Lawyers working for the federal government advance according to the civil service system. Judges usually advance from lower courts to higher courts either in terms of the matters that are decided or in terms of the level—local, state, or federal.

Work Environment

Law offices and courtrooms are usually pleasant—and busy—places to work. Lawyers also spend much of their time in law libraries or record rooms, in the homes and offices of clients, and sometimes in the jail cells of clients or prospective witnesses. Many lawyers never work in a courtroom. Unless they are directly involved in litigation, they may never perform at a trial.

Some courts—such as small claims, family, or surrogate courts—may have evening hours for the convenience of the community. Criminal arraignments may be held at any time of the day or night. Court hours for most lawyers and judges are usually regular business hours, with a one-hour lunch break. Lawyers often work long hours, spending evenings and weekends preparing cases and working with clients. In addition, a lawyer must keep up with the latest developments in the profession. Also, it takes a long time to become a qualified lawyer, and it may be difficult to earn an adequate living until the lawyer gets enough experience to become an established private-practice lawyer.

Lawyers who work in law firms must often work grueling hours to advance in the firm. Spending long weekend hours doing research and interviewing people should be expected.

Earnings

Incomes generally increase as a lawyer gains experience and becomes better known. The beginning lawyer in solo practice may barely make ends meet for the first few years. In 1996, according to the National Association for Law Placement, the starting salary for federal government lawyers was approximately $34,500. Average starting salaries for lawyers in business was nearly $45,000. The top graduates from the best law schools earned more than $80,000 a year.

Salaries for experienced lawyers vary depending on

the type, size, and location of their employers. The 1998 average for lawyers in private industry was about $60,000 annually, although some senior partners earned well over $1 million a year. General attorneys in the federal government were paid about $78,200. Patent attorneys in the federal government averaged around $81,600.

According to the Administrative Office of the U.S. Courts, in 1998, federal district court judges averaged $136,700; federal circuit court judges, $145,000. The chief justice of the United States earned $175,400, while associate justices of the Supreme Court earned $167,900. A survey conducted by the National Center for State Courts reports the 1997 salary average for state intermediate appellate court judges was $103,700; state associate justices earned $105,100.

Outlook

The demand for lawyers is expected to grow as fast as the average through the year 2008. However, record numbers of law-school graduates have created strong competition for jobs, even though the number of graduates has begun to level off. Continued population growth, typical business activities, and increased numbers of legal cases involving health care, environmental, and sexual-harassment issues, among others, will create a steady demand for lawyers. Law services will be more accessible to the middle-income public with the popularity of prepaid legal services and clinics. While employment growth is expected to be only average, the U.S. Department of Labor predicts that 119,000 new positions will be added between the years 1998 and 2008—a 16 percent increase.

The top 10 percent of the graduating seniors of the country's best law schools will have no trouble finding salaried positions in well-known law firms in the next few decades. They will also find work on legal staffs of corporations, in government agencies, and in law schools. Lawyers in solo practice will find it hard to earn a living until their practice is fully established. Their best opportunities exist in small towns or in the suburbs of large cities.

Graduates with average class standings and those from lesser-known schools may have difficulty in getting the best positions. Banks, insurance companies, real-estate firms, government agencies, and other organizations often hire law graduates for administrative, managerial, and business work. Legal positions in the armed forces are also available.

Employment of judges is expected to grow more slowly through the year 2008, according to the U.S. Department of Labor. Judges who retire, however, will have to be replaced. There may be an increase in judges in cities with large population growth, but competition will be high for such openings.

TO LEARN MORE ABOUT LAWYERS AND JUDGES

Books

Allen, Robert A. *William Jennings Bryan: Golden-Tongued Orator.* Milford, Mich.: Mott Media, 1992.

Bayer, Linda N. *Ruth Bader Ginsberg.* Broomall, Penn.: Chelsea House, 2000.

Cornelius, Kay. *The Supreme Court.* Broomall, Penn.: Chelsea House, 2000.

James, Lesley. *Women in Government: Politicians, Lawmakers, Law Enforcers.* Austin, Tex.: Raintree/Steck-Vaughn, 2000.

Kent, Deborah. *Thurgood Marshall and the Supreme Court.* Danbury, Conn.: Children's Press, 1997.

Lommel, Cookie. *Johnnie Cochran.* Broomall, Penn.: Chelsea House, 1999.

McGurn, Barrett. *America's Court: The Supreme Court and the People.* Golden, Colo.: Fulcrum Publishing, 1997.

Websites

American Bar Association

http://www.abanet.org

For information about law school accreditation, continuing legal education, information about the law, programs to assist lawyers and judges in their work, and initiatives to improve the legal system for the public

Association of American Law Schools

http://www.aals.org

For information on workshops and seminars held by this association of 162 law schools

Federal Bar Association

http://fedbar.org

Provides information for law students, new and experienced attorneys, and judges from all over the country

Harvard Law School

http://www.law.harvard.edu/

For information about the oldest law school in the United States

Legal Research on the Internet

http://www.law.onu.edu/internet/

Provides an introduction to many resources used by lawyers and their staffs

Supreme Court of the United States

http://www.supremecourtus.gov/

The official site of the Supreme Court

U.S. Court of Appeals for the Federal Circuit
http://www.fedcir.gov
For information, recent decisions, and notices of the United States Court of Appeals for the Federal Circuit

U.S. Department of Justice
http://www.usdoj.gov/index.html
The official site of this government agency

Where to Write
American Bar Association
Information Services
750 North Lake Shore Drive
Chicago, IL 60611

Association of American Law Schools
1201 Connecticut Avenue, N.W., Suite 800
Washington, DC 20036-2605

Federal Bar Association
Student Services
2215 M Street, N.W.
Washington, DC 20037

U.S. Court of Appeals for the Federal Circuit
717 Madison Place, N.W.
Washington, DC 20439

TO LEARN MORE ABOUT SANDRA DAY O'CONNOR

Books

Bentley, Judith. *Justice Sandra Day O'Connor*. New York: Julian Messner, 1983.

Deegan, Paul J. *Sandra Day O'Connor*. Edina, Minn.: Abdo and Daughters, 1992.

Gherman, Beverly. *Sandra Day O'Connor: Justice for All*. New York: Viking, 1991.

Herda, D. J. *Sandra Day O'Connor: Independent Thinker*. Springfield, N.J.: Enslow Publishers, 1995.

Holland, Gini. *Sandra Day O'Connor*. Austin, Tex.: Raintree/Steck-Vaughn, 1997.

Huber, Peter William. *Sandra Day O'Connor*. New York: Chelsea House, 1990.

McElroy, Lisa Tucker, with Courtney O'Connor. *Meet My Grandmother: She's a Supreme Court Justice*. Brookfield, Conn.: Millbrook Press, 2000.

Websites

National Women's Hall of Fame: Sandra Day O'Connor

http://www.greatwomen.org/ocnnor.htm

A brief biography from the National Women's Hall of Fame

Nine Supreme Individualists: A Guide to the Conversation

http://www.washingtonpost.com/ wp-srv/national/longterm/supcourt/stories/wp042898.htm

Brief biographical sketches of the nine justices provided by the *Washington Post.*

Sandra Day O'Connor

http://supct.law.cornell.edu/supct/justices/ oconnor.bio.html

Biographical data provided by Cornell Law School; includes links to a list of her recent U.S. Supreme Court decisions.

Sandra Day O'Connor: Associate Justice of the Supreme Court

http://www2.lucidcafe.com/lucidcafe/library/96mar/ oconnor.html

Substantial biographical details as well as links to related information

INTERESTING PLACES TO VISIT

Stanford University
Stanford, California 94305
650/723-2300

Supreme Court of the United States
One First Street, NE
Washington, DC 20543
202/479-3030

INDEX

Page numbers in *italics* indicate illustrations.

ABOUT THE
AUTHOR

Jean Kinney Williams grew up in Ohio and lives there now with her husband and four children. She studied journalism in college and, in addition to writing, enjoys reading, volunteering at church, and spending time with her family. She is the author of *Matthew Henson: Polar Adventurer* (Franklin Watts), as well a four books in the American Religious Experience series (Watts). This is her first book for Ferguson Publishing Co.